ROAR
LIKE ME!

by SONIA MARIA

Copyright © 2022 Sonia M Webster
All rights reserved under International and Pan-American Copyright Conventions.

No part of this publication may be reproduced, stored in a retrieval system or transmitted in any form or any means, electronic, mechanical, photocopying, recording or otherwise without the prior written permission of the copyright owner.

Contact us at roadreefpress@gmail.com

Library of Congress Control Number: 2022919583

Summary: Illustrations and rhyming text are used to introduce children to different animals and invite them to mimic the sounds made by each for interactive play. [1. Stories in rhyme; 2. Animals – Fiction; 3. Birds – Fiction; 4. Animals sounds]

ISBN: Paperback 978-1-915695-06-2;
Hardcover 978-1-915695-07-9;
Electronic 978-1-915695-08-6

Printed and distributed in the United States.

For Elizabeth and Enzo

Love you lots!

Lion

I am king of the jungle.
I walk tall and free.
Join my pride and roar like me!

Elephant

I am the biggest land
animal you will ever see.
Raise your trunk and trumpet like me!

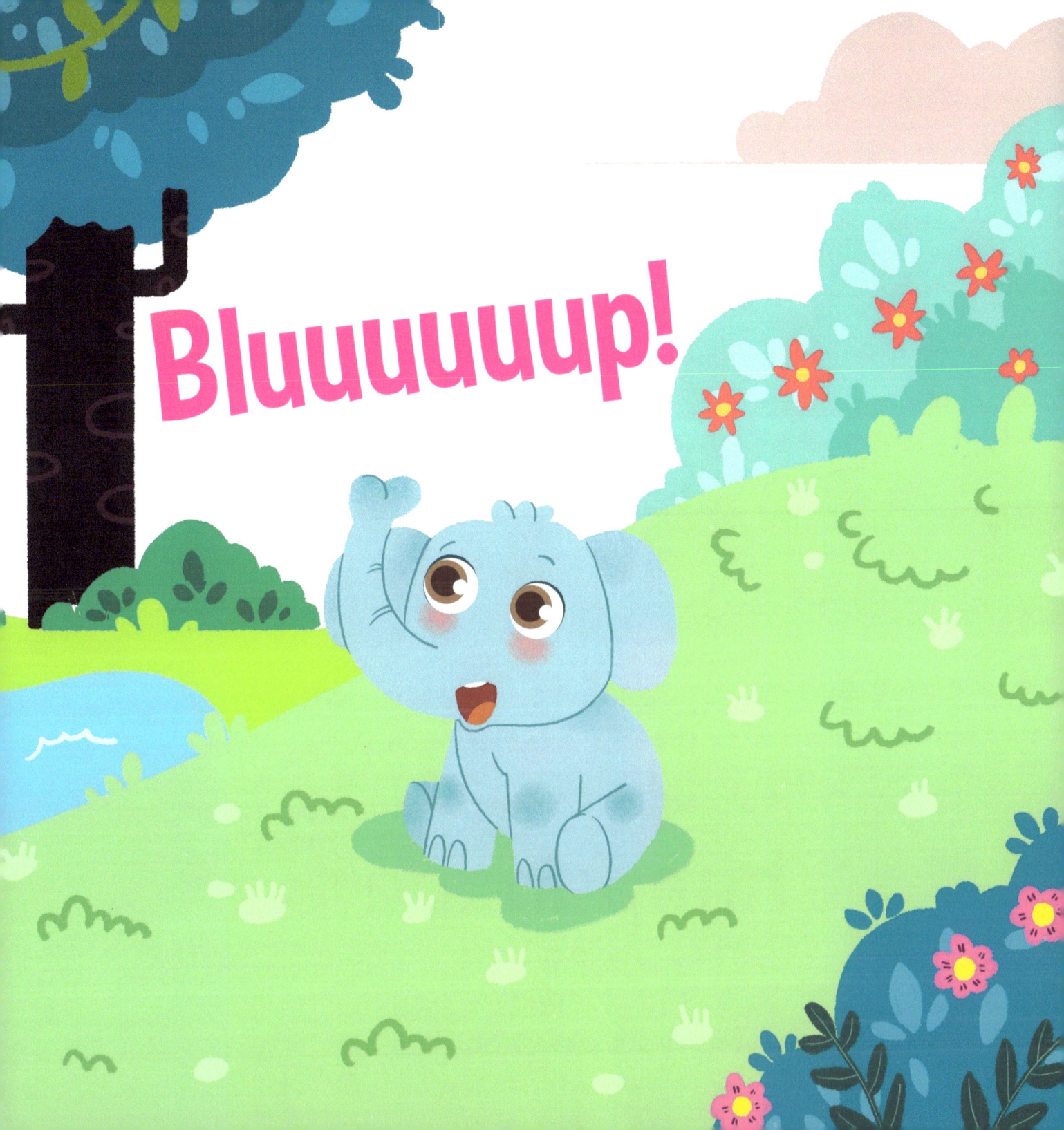

Chimpanzee

I'm a jungle acrobat.
I like to swing and love to chat.
Wave your arms and chant like me!

Snake

I can slither quietly,
through the grass and up a tree.
Lift your head and hiss like me!

Eagle

I soar in the sky
with great majesty.
Raise your voice and screech like me!

Wolf

I sing to the moon
in sweet harmony.
Lift your head and howl like me!

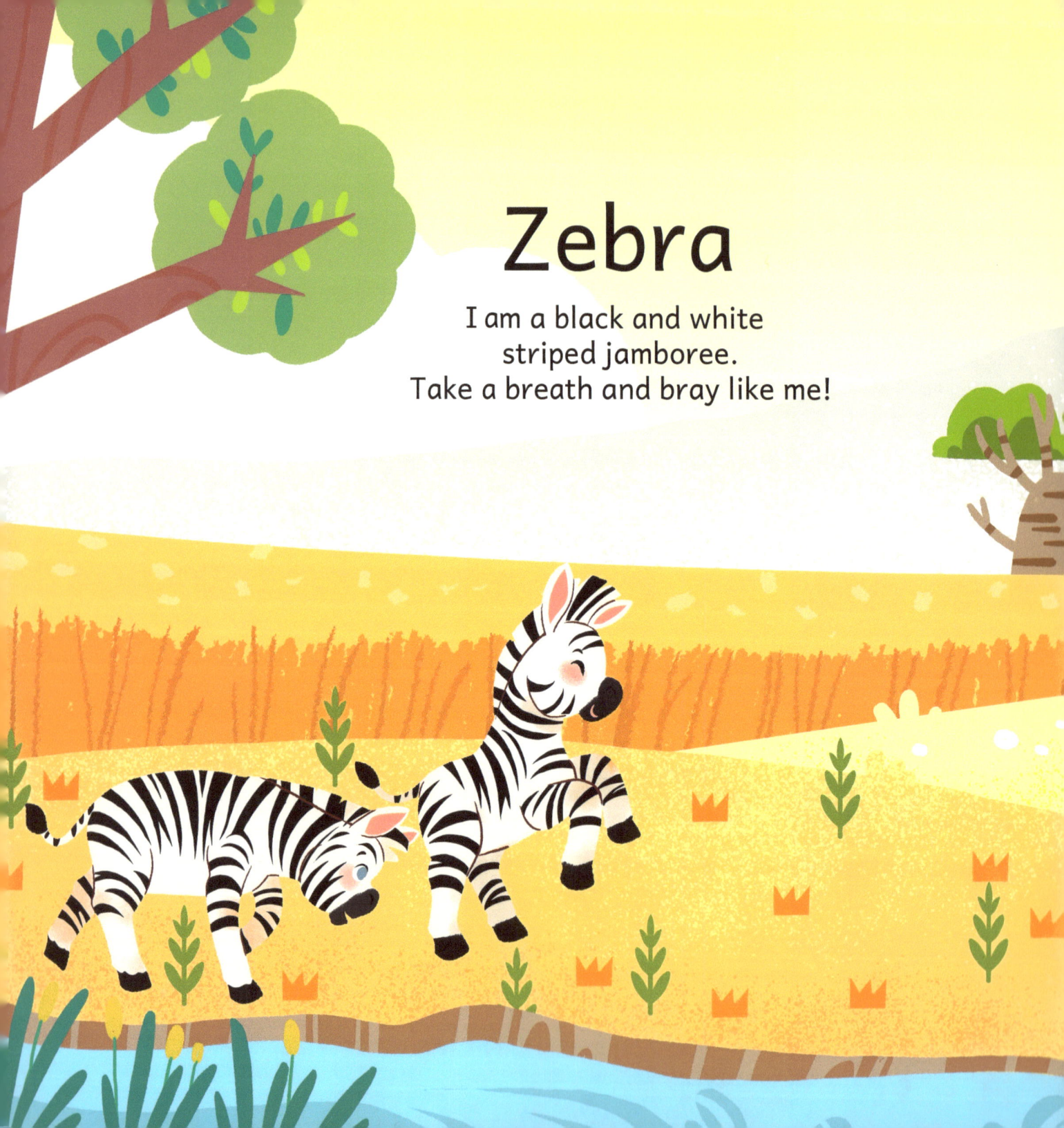

Zebra

I am a black and white
striped jamboree.
Take a breath and bray like me!

Hyena

I sometimes sound like
I am laughing with glee.
Join the fun and cackle like me!

Parrot

I am as colourful as a rainbow and as noisy as can be. Move your head and squawk like me!

Baby

I am a warm and cuddly bundle
as I dream so peacefully.
Close your eyes and sleep like me!

Shhhhhhhhh!

www.ingramcontent.com/pod-product-compliance
Lightning Source LLC
Chambersburg PA
CBHW040024130526
44590CB00036B/86